Join 'The Club'

A Journey for aspiring leaders!

This book is dedicated to my daughters who provide the light in my life and my motivation.

To the many wonderful people who have honored me with the privilege to coach, mentor and support them through their various journeys.

To all the believers in my life, friends, and family, who have provided the sparks to continue each day.

Thank you all!

Chapters:

Chapter 1: The Club

Elyse Jones walked into the main hall of a resort in sunny San Diego, smiling ear to ear, bursting with excitement. She arrived at the annual sales planning and team building off-site for the sales managers at Mech Corp, a well-established manufacturer of various electronic and mechanical components with over seventy offices worldwide. As a new Sales manager, a little over two months into her new role at the Pittsburgh, Pennsylvania branch, she was eager to experience an event widely touted as the key event of the sales leader's year.

Since 1985, Mech Corp has hosted this sales leadership off-site and since it has been a cornerstone of the organization. Annually, the team retreats to an off-site location, typically a resort, where the sales leaders can relax, socialize, and learn. The sales managers lead teams of about twelve sales agents; thus, the event focused on sales planning activities, team buildings, trainings, keynote speakers, networking with other leaders across the organization to learn how to better manage and lead. In addition to the educational opportunities, the major event off-site is the Platinum Performer Club.

The Platinum Performer Club consists of the top five sales managers within Mech Corp for the prior fiscal year. To ensure they receive the highest recognition, the award ceremony is held on the first night of the event. By being early in the program, other leaders within Mech Corp would have the opportunity to both congratulate the winners and learn from them throughout the next four days. Each Platinum Performer, better known as 'The Club', not only received respect, but they also received a seven-day paid vacation to a tropical location and a ten-thousand-dollar bonus. Elyse had always heard of 'The Club' as a sales agent and had dreamed of one day being recognized as a top performer.

Elyse, not knowing what to fully expect, was happy to spot Jimmy Choo, another sales manager from the Pittsburgh branch, across the room. Elyse decided to walk over to sit with him.

"Hi Jimmy!" Elyse said with joy, still overwhelmed by the initial impression of the event. "Isn't this something else?"

"Hi Elyse, welcome to the off-site." Jimmy replied with a lack of enthusiasm that Elyse noticed immediately. Jimmy, who had been in leadership with Mech Corp for over four years as a sales manager and two as a sales agent, had experienced the off-site before and did not share the excitement. Elyse decided to try and break the ice.

"It would be great to be a member of 'The Club'" Elyse said with wide eyed ambition.

Jimmy's response did not show the same passion Elyse expected. "I guess it would be nice" he replied sarcastically while rolling his eyes.

Elyse was taken aback by Jimmy's attitude towards this universally recognized achievement. This is a goal that she believed everyone in the sales leadership team would want to achieve. Elyse failed to understand why someone in leadership wouldn't be more excited for the possibility of being in 'The Club', her curiosity broke the silence.

"Why do you say it like that Jimmy? I think it would be great to be recognized for a job well done and seen by my peers as the best of us! Don't you want to be part of 'The Club'?"

Jimmy replied, "The leaders who earn the recognition of the Platinum Performer Club are deplorable, they treat their staff terribly and drive only towards the company goals. They do not care about their staff; they push and push until their staff either gives up and quits or will do anything to get a sale... and I mean anything. If you care about your staff and you sell with integrity, you never seem to do better than those who care only about the numbers."

Elyse was shocked that Jimmy felt this way. She started her career as a sales agent at Mech Corp two years ago and never felt her manager treated her well and she was able to make her individual goals as a sales agent. While reflecting, she realized her manager Susan never made the Platinum Performer Club nor spoke about wanting to make 'The Club'. Could Jimmy be onto something? She was determined to find out what it took to be part of 'The Club'. In that moment she decided what better way to do so than to meet with the five members of the Platinum Performer Club from this year, speak with them and find out how they lead their teams and got into 'The Club'!

The first evening of the offsite started off with a leadership mingle, no agendas, just grab your name tag that included your location and connect with other sales leaders. After walking around for a bit, Elyse and Jimmy found a table and sat down. Elyse was looking forward to meeting managers from all over the country during the next four days, however, was glad to be with someone familiar at the start of the event. A few moments later Elyse spotted her former manager Susan and waved to her to come to the table.

Susan looked in her direction and started to walk towards her and Jimmy. Susan Cunningham carried herself with extreme confidence, she was one of the most tenured managers in Mech Corp for twelve years. Elyse did not know a lot about Susan's past beyond her experiences since joining the company.

"Hi Elyse, how are you enjoying your first off site?" Susan said pleasantly knowing how overwhelming this event could be for a new manager.

"It is going great, it is amazing to have so many talented leaders in one place, I am looking forward to the keynote speakers and the team building sessions… and of course the Platinum Performer presentation tonight!

Susan's enthusiastic demeanor changed instantly, "Oh, the Club presentation huh… it is the same old story every year."

Elyse was taken aback, first Jimmy now Susan, both leaders who she felt performed well and had good tenure, leaders who she looked up to from her home office. Elyse started to wonder if there was something to what Jimmy had said and decided to press forward with questioning Susan.

"Susan, what do you mean by it is the same story every year?"

Susan took a sip of her drink, looked down at the floor to muster up the courage to speak her mind. After a moment she looked Elyse straight in the eyes with a look of concern as she expressed her opinion about 'The Club'.

"Each year the pageantry gets more elaborate, executive leaders speak about their teams' successes and their praise floods the venue while they announce this year's 'Club' members. When the five winners are on stage, Peter will ask them what they feel is the single most important action they have taken that led to their success as a leader. One by one they spout off common sense topics that we all know and make it seem like it is an astonishingly new revelation. We toast our victors, and the night goes on."

Elyse did not know how to react. She could not believe the tone of Susan's comment, it seemed as if Susan had some jealousy or anger towards the winners. Elyse worked for Susan when she was a sales agent and had only but great experiences. She decided to dive into the conversation further to see what she could uncover.

"Susan, are you saying there is no magic formula to being successful and they just do the same things we are trained to do day in and day out, yet get to the top out of luck?"

Susan grinned at the question and stated "they say they do the same things we are trained to do; yet we all know they don't treat their teams well and will do anything for a sale. You are new to your role; give it time and you will see how cutthroat it is. People like us are not meant for 'The Club'; we care too much our people, and we have ethical standards."

Now this was truly disheartening, Susan and Jimmy had similar messages, how could this be? Elyse decided to ask another question as she could see Susan was not enjoying this line of questioning.

"Susan, have you ever made 'The Club'?"

Without hesitation Susan looked around to ensure no one was listening into their conversation.

"Elyse, I have never even been close to making 'The Club.' I have met our company goals and KPIs, yet every year there are many managers who have met or exceeded theirs as well. I am too focused on my team members, and I don't want to burn them out. While meeting our organizational goals is one of my focus points, I don't try to push harder than meeting the goals. Once our team hits the goals we are set, pushing harder will only hurt the team."

She sat there for a moment thinking about her time on Susan's team. Susan was a great boss; she was a leader and followed the rules. Elyse always felt supported on the team and exceeded her individual goals, however other team members did not hit their goals. There were some sales agents who exceeded, a few who met and a few who did not. Overall, that came out to a team win and that was the goal. Susan provided coaching and support to all, however looking back Elyse realized it was her own internal ambition that pushed her to exceed, not Susan's encouragement.

Elyse was more curious than ever to understand how The Club members achieved the success they did. Was it because they didn't play by the rules and cut corners, ignoring ethical principles? Was it because their teams' worked hours on end with no work life balance, exceeding in effort over other teams? Based on how Susan and Jimmy described it, Elyse didn't know what to think.

The time finally came, the Platinum Performer Club awards were about to be announced. Just like Susan described, the ceremony was grand with a wall sized screen projecting past winners to upbeat music, blue laser lights beaming across the ceiling darting back and forth across the room and an atmosphere of intense anticipation.

One by one members of the executive leadership team took turns providing details on their specific team's achievements during the year. This was a sales team event; however, each executive leader shared their teams' successes to provide context to the impact of other teams in the organization. Elyse was excited to learn more about the overall direction of Mech Corp. She was happy the executive leaders took the time to meet with the sales leadership team at their off site and share their successes.

The Chief Financial Officer provided details about the finance team's improvements, specifically how account receivable has seen a twenty improvement in on time payments. The Head of People spoke about the benefit and wellness plan improvements her team implemented leading to a fifteen increase in employee satisfaction scores. Lastly the Chief Operating Officer spoke of his team's expansion into three new cities where offices would be opening within the next six months.

Now was the time for Peter Lytle to take the stage to share the successes of the sales team. Peter, the Chief Sales Officer at Mech Corp, was a tall man with stoic features, dressed in a sharp business suit. His presence commanded the attention of the crowd. Elyse was looking around the room and she could tell Peter was in charge. With his deep bellowing voice, he approached the podium, there was silence as the audience waited for him to break the stillness of the room.

"Welcome all! Before we get started, I want to stress, your success in this role will be measured by how well you lead your team to grow and meet organizational sales goals and the relationships you build with our business partners and customers. This off-site provides an opportunity for all of us to learn new skills and sharpen our swords. I excited you all here and to celebrate as a leadership family."

Every year Peter kept on theme, adjusting the wording of his message, however always focusing on achievement, accountability, and relationships.

Elyse had seen Peter in the office, and he had spoken to the teams over video conferences quarterly. After hearing this powerful introduction, she was eager to hear more as she wanted to grow her career within Mech Corp. She felt this off-site was a huge opportunity for her to learn and grow.

"Last year was one of our most profitable years at Mech Corp. Our revenue exceeded four million on a new sales goal of two million. Our profit margin improved year-over-year by and our customer retention has never been higher. With that success comes growth as we are expanding into five new markets in the next year!"

The room filled with cheers and applause; Elyse was energized by the positivity in the room. Peter took a moment to take in the accolades and as the crowd's roar died down, he led into the awards.

"While most of our sales teams met or outperformed, we take this opportunity to recognize the top five sales teams from the past year. These teams could not have achieved the heights they did without the five leaders who will soon be on stage before you. It is my pleasure to announce this year's Platinum Performer Club Members!"

At this moment Elyse was on her tippy toes to get a better look at the stage as everyone was standing and cheering. The excitement of the moment as a spectator was exhilarating, imagine what it would be like to be one of the five Elyse though as she felt the energy of the moment.

"Our first member hails from Nashville. One of our most tenured team members, she has been with Mech Corp for ten years, the last five as a sales manager and has been in the Club the last two years, please give it up for Lisa Townsley!"

"Our next member is the first member of the Club to make it by managing three distinct locations. His first trip to the Club was five years ago with the Miami branch, then four years ago with the Tampa Bay branch, now after a three-year hiatus from the Club, he is back with the Miami branch, let's celebrate Javier Santos!"

"The next member of the Platinum Club is no stranger to being on this stage, as a Club member two years ago he took some time off to join our national training team and last year rejoined our sales management staff in Seattle. Let's hear it for Erik Connell!"

"Being a newcomer to this club is no small feat, this year we have one new member, a rising star. She started her career with Mech Corp this prior year as a sales manager in our Boston branch and has led her team to amazing sales results and has the highest customer satisfaction scores across the organization. Please show your appreciation for Monica Tan!"

"The final member of this year's Platinum Club is also our top sales team leader each of the last five years! Each year he has broken his previous team organizational sales records and set new ceilings for Mech Corp. Representing our final spot in this year's Club and the Chicago branch; Steven Kingham!"

Elyse clapped as hard as she could, the room was erupting with excitement to celebrate 'The Club' members for this year. As she looked over, Peter moved off to the far side of the stage now so the winners could stand front and center. She observed Peter's look of pride, like a father whose child just got a full scholarship to an Ivy League school. Next Elyse looked over to Susan who was standing with Jimmy, they were unenthusiastically clapping as to fit in with the crowd without providing genuine support to those on stage. The applause kept going and Elyse was excited about what was to come; each Club member would briefly speak about what they felt was the most important attribute to getting them on stage!

Chapter 2: How did you get here?

After the five winners were announced, the applause continued for a few minutes then the crowd settled down into their seats. Elyse sat on the edge of her chair, leaning forward, anticipating lessons that would help take her career to the next level. The podium was removed, and the stage was set up in a very relaxed fireside style chat, with a long couch and three sofa chairs in preparation for the discussion. As the applause ended, each of 'The Club' members turned to find a seat, Peter pulled the microphone from the podium, sat down in a sofa chair, and kicked off the round table.

"Congratulations, I am so proud of you all. As you know each year after we reveal the five members of 'The Club', we ask that each of our winners to briefly discuss what they feel has been the most pivotal skill set or behavior that contributed towards their success in the prior year. While this is not an all-inclusive list of successful traits, it serves as a consistent reminder that each sales leader must lean in on their strengths and work towards impacting their teams. With that said, Lisa, can you get us started?"

Lisa was smiling from ear to ear, her eyes sparkling in the spotlight which was now focused on her. Everyone in the audience could see her overwhelming joy of being back on stage and in 'The Club.' As she held the microphone close the room went silent in anticipation of the knowledge Lisa was about to share. Elyse looked over at Jimmy who was still sitting at the table, he had a neutral posture, not as interested as she was, however being respectful of the leaders on stage. She peered at Susan who had a look of disgust towards her peers on stage. Elyse, eager to start learning, pulled out her notebook to take notes.

"Thank you, Peter, and thank you to everyone for all your hard work and focus on our customers and our teams. When I look back to the past year and think what the main driver for the success of my team, I can say without a doubt it is the wonderful culture that has been built within the team. My team works as a single unit, always there to help one another, they lift each other up when times are tough and celebrate all the wins. They continually approach each day with a positive attitude knowing together they can do anything. When things may not go our way, we know together we can round the corner and make an impact on our customers and one another. The culture of my team influences our interactions with internal partners and customers, which makes every day enjoyable."

Attentively listening, Elyse was surprised at how obvious a great culture on a team will impact their success. Lisa's comments were brief and concise, Elyse knew what she should focus on this topic. She wrote the word "Culture" in her notebook with a few key words. She gazed back up to the stage as Lisa gently handed the microphone back to Peter.

"Thank you, Lisa, and congratulations again! Culture plays an important role in all that we do, having a great team culture is critical and I would suggest everyone make sure to ask themselves; is the culture on my team what I would like it to be, and if not, how can I change it for the better?". Next let's hear from Javier on what he feels has led to the success of his team."

As Peter handed the microphone to Javier and the crowd began to clap again, Elyse looked around and noticed her branch mates were still not as attentive or enthusiastic as she was. Elyse began wondering how many leaders across the organization felt the way she did and wanted to be on that stage next year or how many of the sales leaders in the crowd felt the same as Susan. The thought of being up there next year and being a leader others looked up to refocused Elyse as the room grew quiet as Javier motioned to speak.

"Wow this is an honor, I missed being up here on stage being able to share with all of you the main reason my team has been so successful, regardless of the location and regardless of the time I have with each team. One word, motivation! My team takes on each day with a passion that is only present when there is consistent motivation. While the personal motivation of each team member varies, the focus of that motivation is to improve on the experience we deliver for our customers and on the team meeting their goals for one another. A motivated team will rise to the occasion every time! Thank you."

Elyse was again surprised that something so simple would be a factor expressed in this part of the program. She thought to herself there is no magic formula to motivation since all sales folks are already motivated to meet their goals. With confident intent Elyse wrote "Motivation" and some key points in her notebook. As Javier was handing the microphone back to Peter, Elyse felt more confident that she could be a part of 'The Club' next year.

"Always a pleasure having you up on stage, Javier" Peter bellowed. "Motivation is one of my favorite topics, we all need to look internally to find our personal motivation. Next up is another familiar face to all, a superstar sales leader turned trainer turned superstar sales leader, let's hear what Erik felt was the major contributor to his team's success."

Elyse was eager to hear what Eric had to say, as a national trainer everyone knew Erik. He would travel the country facilitating continuing education to front line sales staff and the management staff. When Elyse joined Mech Corp Erik was the first person she interacted with those initial two weeks, he was very open to teaching everyone around him and Elyse had on more than one occasion reached out for guidance after exiting training. With her notes app in hand Elyse turned to give Erik her full attention.

Being a natural speaker, Erik stood up rather than taking the fireside approach and walked to the front of the stage with poise and confidence. As he began to speak the whole facility again turned quiet with a level of respect and eagerness to hear his wisdom. "Thanks Peter and thank you all! I look out and see so many talented leaders across our organization, it is a personal high to be up here speaking about our craft." Erik paused with the self-assurance of a politician, pausing for effect and to collect his thoughts, "There are so many factors that lead to a team's success, with this in mind if I had to pick the most important factor that led to my team's success it would be staff development. There are many forms of staff development across each team in fact, so leaders focus on each individual and their development is critical to the team's success. I have found the amount of attention you provide your staff regarding their professional and personal development; you will see the impact they have on their confidence in all aspects of their role. Thank you."

Elyse quickly wrote "Development" after her earlier notes of "Culture" and "Motivation". Elyse was excited about a colleague she knew was up there and provided a great attribute for her collection. She reflected on her weekly performance reviews with her staff and felt more confident she would be able to gain the skills needed to make 'The Club' next year.

"Thank you, Erik! For those of you who may not know, Erik was a sales agent on one of my teams many years ago and demonstrated that same vigor around developing others around him then as he does now. We appreciate all you do Erik. Our next Club member is Monica, as the newest member to Mech Corp to be up here, tell us what you feel was the main factor to your success this past year?"

Peter handed the microphone to Monica who showed the emotion of the moment on her face. It appeared as if she was surprised to have made 'The Club', however there was a nervousness to her expressions. "Thank you, Peter, it is overwhelming to be part of this wonderful group and to be part of this larger team of amazing leaders. As many of you know I am new to Mech Corp, however you may not know that I was never a sales agent at Mech Corp. I was hired directly as a sales manager. I have many years of experience and the most impactful characteristic I feel led my team to success and me on this stage today is work ethic. As a newcomer getting up to speed was a challenge and having an excellent work ethic helped the most. Being an example for your team and setting the bar high for work ethic, while still maintaining a proper work-life balance is critical. Those who are motivated on your team will emulate your behaviors, so always lead the way, and set an example. Thank you."

Monica's statement around work ethic took Elyse by surprise. Being newer to leadership herself she could relate to the challenge of leading a team for the first time, however there were so many other things she felt were more important to the team than the leader's work ethic and that of their team. With a deep desire to learn more, Elyse wrote "Work Ethic" in her notebook with the hope she will be able to explore what Monica felt work ethic entailed. The room became quiet again as Peter was getting ready to introduce the final member of this year's 'Club'.

"Thank you, Monica, we are so glad to have you in the family. Ensuring our leaders and teams have a good work ethic in both the focus towards getting the tasks done and the methods in which they complete the tasks is a great focus! Finally, we get to Steven. As I mentioned earlier Steven has been the top sales team leader five years straight, it is uncanny how consistent his team delivers." Peter paused as the crowd chuckled a little at his complementary jab. "Demonstrating consistency, Steven has stated 'Knowledge' as his key attribute the last four years, let's see if he brings this level of consistency today." Peter smiled at Steven who was smiling back at him from ear to ear as he grabbed the microphone. The audience again chuckled for a moment as the two shared a respectable glance.

"Thank you, Peter, you know me oh too well. Each year being up here feels like the first time and it is always a highlight of my year. I have not found a more critical skill set than being knowledgeable as a sales leader and as a salesperson. That knowledge spans all of what you do, your products, your people, your customers and beyond. I do not feel I would have been up here any of the past five years without the knowledge that I have. I challenge each of you to continue to seek out and learn all you can about our business. Thank you."

Elyse was in awe, the best-selling team leader in the organization for five years was focused on knowledge, how could this be? As a new sales leader, Elyse understood there was much for her to study and her appetite for learning has always been high, but the team had knowledge bases and one-pagers on products, what more could they need. With a sense of curiosity and more confidence than ever Elyse wrote "Knowledge" into her list of skill sets and quickly turned back to the stage as Peter was about to deliver his final comments.

Peter and Steven exchanged another look of mutual admiration as the baton was again passed to Peter. "Thank you, Steven, it is nice to know how predictable you are." As Peter looked out at the room full of Mech Corp leaders, he paused for a moment and started to close the evening out. "While we only have five leaders on this stage, I am proud of the accomplishments of each of you. Every year is different, it comes with new challenges that we must approach head on. Each year we focus on delivering for our customers and our team members and every year we rise to the challenge. As we wrap up tonight's events think about what you want to take away from our off-site, look at the scheduled events and pick sessions that will help you maximize your time here. Know that the lessons you learn this week will help you continue to grow and impact your team. In case you were unaware, there is a social meet your peers' mixer tonight in the adjacent room, feel free to stop by and meet some of your fellow sales leaders, have a great evening and I will see you all over the next few days!"

"That was inspiring" said Susan in a sarcastic tone. "Each year it is more of the same old message and each year the same 'favorites' make it up there by cutting corners and greasing their way up on stage. Elyse please don't waste your time digging into what they said, you are great at what you do, and you will get there one day!"

Susan's comment, while meant as a compliment, was upsetting to Elyse. Taking a moment to consider how fellow branch leaders felt and how defeating it seemed, she responded in kind. "Thanks Susan, I appreciate the confidence you have in me. I feel we can all learn from the leaders in our company who are leading their teams at a high level."

With that Susan nodded and walked away. Elyse turned to Jimmy with open eyes asking for a different opinion.

"Elyse, do what you feel is best. It is tough year after year to not be part of 'The Club' and I think it has just gotten to Susan over the years. If you feel you can learn then you should, however it isn't an ambition for everyone, make sense?

Elyse was happy that Jimmy had a more positive spin on her ambition. "Thank you, Jimmy, you have a good night!"

The large reception room started to clear out as many of the sales leaders went to the mixer in the other room, while others went back to their rooms to rest up from a long day of travel. Elyse looked down at her notes for a moment and felt optimistic in her goal to be in 'The Club' next year. Elyse felt she was heading in the right direction with these five traits from each leader as to what made them successful. Now the challenge was getting to learn as much as she could from the members of 'The Club' while they are all in one place. Elyse decided to skip the mixer and retire to her room for a night of rest... since tomorrow would be the beginning of her journey.

Chapter 3: Culture

The next morning Elyse awoke to her alarm clock going blaring. Her first thoughts were about the days ahead. Elyse was eager to absorb as much as she could, knowing her team would benefit from all she could learn, and she would develop as a leader. After getting herself ready, Elyse headed to the daily continental breakfast with a spring in her step and a burning desire to learn.

While at breakfast luck, fate or a little of both seemed to be on her side. Sitting alone at a table was Lisa Townsley, one of the members of 'The Club'. Elyse thought to herself this had to be a sign. Never shy, she jumped at the chance to speak with her.

"Hi Lisa, may I sit with you?" Elyse spoke softly, not knowing if Lisa was a morning person and ready to engage in a conversation with a stranger.

"Absolutely, please" Lisa responded with kindness, appearing happy to have someone to sit with.

With a huge smile, Elyse packed on the charm "Thank you, I don't know many of the sales managers here yet. My name is Elyse, nice to meet you."

"Nice to meet you too, I'm Lisa from the Nashville branch. Where are you from"?

"I am with the Pittsburgh branch; I've been in the sales manager role for only a few months but hoping to do well and make it to 'The Club' next year."

With a look of certainty and encouragement, Lisa smiled and responded, "I think that is a great goal and I hope we both make it on stage next year."

Elyse was taken back; Lisa was immediately supportive. She had never been in a situation where a peer who was in direct competition for accolades was so openly encouraging, especially after just meeting them. How could this be? Elyse decided to jump at the chance to ask Lisa questions about her speech last night.

"Thank you, Lisa. I appreciate your take on culture last night, would you mind if I asked some questions, I want to learn as much as I can while I am here?"

Lisa's smile started to move into a curious gaze, she paused for a moment then nodded her head permitting Elyse's curiosity.

"Last night you mentioned 'Culture' as the biggest impact of your team's success, what specifically about culture makes it so important?

Still smiling, Lisa jumped at this opportunity to speak about something she was so passionate about. "Well, you see, culture is all around us, reflected in how each team member treats one another, how they treat their customers and the general environment we work in. It starts with me, and it ends with me."

Elyse was taking notes to ensure the valuable lessons would be close to her on her journey. She looked up and as she did Lisa continued.

"You see Elyse, as the leader of our teams, it is our responsibility to not only build the culture, but we must also maintain and protect it. Tell me, have you ever made a poor hiring decision that impacted your team?"

Elyse quickly responded "I have not, however I do remember a hire that Susan made about a year ago, his name was Chris. When he joined the team things changed instantly."

"How did they change" asked Lisa, with the same curiosity Elyse had in learning about culture.

"Well, he had a lot of sales experience in the industry, which was exciting for our team to get someone who had done the job before, yet he never lived up to his potential. When we had team meetings, he would blame the leads he received, he would blame the marketing department for their strategy, he would blame the technology for being inferior from his last place of employment and would often challenge Susan on our policies and procedures. He would do this in front of everyone, it impacted the confidence we all had in Susan, marketing, technology, and the leads as well. Susan tried to collaborate with him and help him see how successful he could be; however, it didn't work out, two months later he quit."

"When he left, did the team go back to normal operations before he joined the team?" Lisa asked, anticipating the answer.

"No, it took some time, at least three months for the doubt he placed to go away. A few other good employees ended up leaving as well, one even followed Chris to his new place as a sales agent. It took Susan a while to get back to full staff and regain the team's trust."

Just as Elyse finished her statement a light bulb went off and she realized the impact bringing Chris onto the team had on the team culture.

"Do you think if Susan didn't hire Chris the team would have stayed together and been more successful during that period of time?" Elyse asked with uncertainty.

"I can't say for sure. I can say that to ensure your team has the culture you want as a leader; you must know who you are bringing onto the team, how you bring them onto the team and closely engage while the team's culture adjusts to new, or even less people."

"How, how can you be sure the person you are bringing onto your team fits the culture? I was always taught you want diversity on your team."

"You always want diversity, which is one of the most important aspects of culture. You can have diversity and still make hiring selections that fit your team by properly vetting the candidates for a dual fit. Do they fit your team and does your team fit them? When you are interviewing candidates who you are considered for your team, you always want to set realistic expectations with them before they are hired. Set the tone up front so they know what to expect and when they are on-boarded deliver what they expect, specifically around the culture of your team. At the same time be sure to ask the candidate questions that are specific to their past experiences, with examples of how they dealt with situations, so you can get to know their style."

Elyse was writing fast, taking notes on every point. Lisa continued.

"By seeking a dual fit, you are giving the candidate a chance to decline the position and your team and your culture, which is not a bad thing. By asking those specific questions you are giving yourself a chance to pass on the candidate or pass them along to another team if they are a better fit."

"What kind of expectations do you set in these interviews?"

"First, I make sure to tell them the worst part of the role. They will have days with long hours, they will have a sale they are working on for a month that falls through, they will have to chip in on peak sales weeks. Next, I make sure they know we follow a specific process and procedure that has worked for years, we are open to feedback and improvement however they must work in this paradigm for a while to learn our style before suggesting improvements. Lastly, I am always sure to point out how we are a team, we win together, we lose together, we respect each other, and we help each other."

"Do you always get it right?" Elyse asked.

"Not always, but more so than not. After I set those expectations, I ask the candidate if they want to continue the interview process, sometimes they bow out at that moment and the interview is over. I respect that they know themselves well enough to know it isn't a fit. If they wish to proceed, I ask questions specific to the role and their experience, then provide them an opportunity to ask questions. You can tell al lot by the questions they prepare, or don't prepare." Lisa smiled thinking about some of her past experiences."

"Even with that rigor you can still get it wrong, however it is quickly known, and a frank conversation can help ease the situation and bring a resolution. For example, I hired someone on my team nine months ago and she was brilliant in the interview, I outlined my expectations and after the interview I decided to extend an offer to the candidate. She showed up on day one, completed a few days of onboarding and training then pulled me aside. She apologized and decided the job was not a fit for her, she thanked me for the opportunity and left quietly. Because she respected the culture and how I set expectations, she understood the fit was not there, it stung because we had to start the search again, however the team wasn't impacted, culture remained as is."

Lisa took a bite of her bagel while Elyse finished taking notes on the last topic. Elyse was thrilled to get this level of detail, not only about culture but the hiring process. She had no idea the impact of hiring the right or wrong person for a role had such an impact on a team's culture. She waited for Lisa to finish chewing and asked her next question.

"There must be more to building a great culture than making good hiring decisions. What else is there to building culture?"

"When I mentioned in the interview I set expectations, all of those are part of the culture. The way we come together to help one another in the tough times and how we celebrate the good times. Understanding we all need to chip in when we hit the busy peaks in our business cycle to meet the needs of our customers. How we not only follow policies and procedures but are responsible as a team to suggest improvements and better them year over year."

Elyse noticed how Lisa changed the tense of her lesson. When it was about the candidate selection process she used 'I', now she is using 'we' as the descriptor. "Lisa, do you take part in all of those activities you mentioned?"

Lisa nodded, "Yes, as a leader you should never ask anyone on your team to do something you would not be willing to do yourself. There are many members of our team who are better at sales than I ever was, that doesn't mean I can't sit with them when I have some time and make some calls or go on appointments. When we are working extra hours there is always a team leader there to make sure we support one another, and everyone knows we are in this together. We have open forums every quarter to discuss what went well and what we want to improve upon, having open lines of communication is a big part of culture."

"Is there anything else to building a great culture?"

"There is a lot that goes into building a great culture, remember it starts with the leader and ends with the leader. For example, I also strive to have a diversified team so there are many different viewpoints which help drive new thought and innovation. Having a vision of what you want your team's culture to be and working towards that is critical, you ought to start somewhere, why not with your vision. If you do it right, your team will have trust in each other and the culture you have built will take on a life of its own. It may not look or feel exactly like you planned, but the key aspects will be there. It takes time to develop a positive sustaining culture and you can't do it without trust."

When she was younger, Elyse learned a little about trust. Her parents had told her trust is like a credit score, it takes time to build up and can be broken very easily. "Any tips on building trust?"

"Do what you say you will do, hold team members accountable so it is fair across the board, engage them in improving the department and be transparent and honest. Understand that trust is built differently with everyone, some members on your team may trust quickly, others may take more time. The key is once you build it don't lose it!"

Elyse looked up and realized the room started to empty for the first team builder of the day.

"Thank you, Lisa, so much for the lesson. I can't wait to get back to start building my team's culture. You have helped tremendously!"

"You are welcome, you can reach out any time. There is a lot more to culture, but this should be a good start. I am happy to help. I look forward to hearing some progress reports along the way."

"You bet!" Elyse replied with enthusiasm.

They both stood up, feeling a sense of accomplishment, Lisa was happy to have assisted a new leader at Mech Corp by passing along some valuable knowledge while Elyse was overjoyed to have received such a wealth of knowledge that she could apply to her team.

With one down and four to go, Elyse felt a sense of confidence that she would be able to meet with all 'The Club' members over the next three days. As they exited, they joined the larger group for the planned activities of the day.

Chapter 4: Development

After an eventful first day of team building and training sessions, most everyone was attending dinner at the resort, Elyse decided it would be a good opportunity to continue her journey and meet with another member of 'The Club'. As she entered the dining room her eyes surveyed the room, probing the bar, looking at the buffet tables and finally at the dinner tables. After a few moments, she spotted Erik sitting by himself at a faraway dinner table. It was curious that such a known entity at Mech Corp would be sitting by himself, Elyse thought this was a sign and headed towards him.

"Hi Erik" Elyse said with a smile.

"Oh, Hi Elyse, how are you doing?" Eric responded with his typical charming smile.

"I am doing great, today was amazing, I learned so much and met a lot of new people. How about you?"

Eric chuckled "That is exactly what this off-site was meant to do, glad you are open to new lessons. I am well, just a bit tired, my flight was delayed, and I almost missed the presentation."

"I had no clue; well, you look alert to me" Elyse responded in kind.

"Thank you, please join me."

As Elyse sat down, she noticed Erik had a notebook that he may have been writing in before she walked over. "I am sorry, were you working?" she asked.

"Always working, but this isn't the work you think. This is my staff journal."

Intrigued by this concept, Elyse decided to dive in. "Ok, I'll bite... what is a 'staff journal'?

"This is the most important piece to my success; it is a journal that I use to keep track of how I can help develop people who I care about. It helps me keep track of what we are working on and what the responsible actions are."

Elyse somehow walked right into the conversation she was hoping to have. During the presentation Erik mentioned the development of his staff and this was the secret to his success and here he is, still focused on his team's development.

"Really, that is great. How many Mech Corp agents are in your journal?"

"I don't know the number, and the journal has other people in it beyond Mech Corp, but a majority of the folks in the journal are trainees, team members and peers who I try to help as best I can."

"Others?" Elyse said with a puzzled look.

"Absolutely!" Erik responded in a positive tone. "There is no better feeling in this world than helping someone achieve their goals, either within our organization or elsewhere. The next best feeling is helping them on that journey!"

Now this was impressive; Elyse had never heard of anyone taking an interest like this in people who didn't work for them, she needed to learn more.

"Are the people in your book mainly those that have been in your trainings?"

"Some of them are, some of them stem from my previous employer, some of them are college friends and a few of them are neighbors who asked me for help. You see, while I am back in a sales leadership role, my passion is helping others learn. You can say I am a life-long educator who provides a dose of reality to my students."

Erik sat back with a grin, knowing that this statement would peak Elyse's interest. Elyse was confused and more ambitious to understand Erik's take on development.

"What do you mean a dose of reality?"

"Before I get to that, let me ask you a few questions. What has you so interested in this topic?"

Elyse looked at Erik with sincerity and took a moment to gather her thoughts. "I want to be part of 'The Club', that is a goal of mine. I am hoping to learn from you and the other Club members what it takes to be successful. If you feel a 'staff journal' is a key to success, then I want to know all about it!"

"Tell me, do you want to help others or just yourself?"

This question took Elyse by surprise, why would Erik think she did not want to help others? "Of course, I want to help everyone on my team reach their potential."

"What if, after I teach you about the development of others, you find out one of your team members doesn't want to be successful at Mech Corp. What will you do?"

Elyse was more confused than ever, why would someone not want to be successful at their job? Their role as a sales agent could lead to a distinguished career, future roles in management and a greater income.

"I never thought about someone not wanting to be successful at their job. If that happened, I would still help them, I may have some questions as to why and try to get them to be good at their job... but I would still help them."

"That is the answer I was looking for!" Erik stared with joy. "Ok, let me ask a few more questions to get a baseline of what you are doing now. When you have a one-on-one with your team members, what do you talk about?"

"We talk about their performance since our last one-on-one, typically review if they are hitting their KPIs and if we have time, we may go over the details of some failed sales visits or calls."

Erik had a grin like that of a child who was about to pull a prank on their friends. "Tell me, where did you learn that style of one-on-one?"

"No one taught me how to do them really, I just started doing them like all my managers have done with me in the past. I figured that was what worked with me so that is what I should do with my staff." Elyse said with confidence.

"I am sorry to hear that Elyse, this is why standard manager training should be required for all leaders."

Elyse had a puzzled look, why did Erik apologize? "Why are you apologizing Erik?"

"As you know developing people is my passion, which includes all staff. Manager training is not included in the training program and the impact trickles down to their staff. When I deliver one-on-one training for new managers, I start by setting the tone for three specific topics that all managers should discuss in their one-on-ones. You mentioned that format of one-on-ones worked for you when you were a sales agent, do you feel what works for you works for everyone?"

This was a simple question with an obvious answer. "No, I understand that we are individuals and what works for one person may not work for another."

"Well said, we are individuals. Now let's think about the content of your one-on-one's, does your staff know their performance before they meet with you?"

"Absolutely!" Elyse was quick to answer. "Every day we send out sales progress reports to the team, highlighting top performances for the prior day and current week. I also meet with each team member throughout the week to go over performance specifically and check in throughout the week."

"Why then do you again talk about performance with your staff on their one-on-ones?"

Elyse took a moment to think about how she would respond, no one had pointed out the duplication of topics before. After a minute of silence Elyse was ready to respond.

"I never thought about it like that before, it is to make sure they know that I care about them, and I want them to be successful. To me success is about hitting their goals."

"Showing that you genuinely care about them, that is essential. Focusing on their success is also important. However, the goals of the organization may not be what they see as their personal success. What are your thoughts about asking your staff in their one-on-ones about what success is to them?"

Again, Elyse paused to reflect on the question. As a new manager she has simply imitated what her previous managers had done, what she had observed over the years. This was a whole new way to look at supporting her staff.

"I think that would be an interesting question to ask each of them." she said with a smile.

"How so?" Erik responded.

"Well, it would be curious to find out if they feel success is the same as what I feel success is in their role. We set out goals for them to hit, seems clear to me."

"I agree, it seems clear on what the goal is, however, have you ever asked your staff how you can help them be successful in what they are currently doing?"

"I have when we are going over performance results or if I am just checking in with the team, you know to see how I can help."

"That is good! Now let's apply that thinking to the first topic 'How can I as your leader help you in your current role?' That simple question, without reviewing data prior will lead to some great conversations!"

Elyse thought about it for a moment, how is that different than what she is doing now besides not reviewing data? "But Erik, don't I need to show them the data before we ask that question to understand how I can help?"

"Before I answer, let me remind you that you already review their performance in a few different ways a few different times through the week, do you think they are unaware or forgot how they are doing in such a short time?"

"No, I see what you are getting at, they know their performance and they know the score."

"Exactly, so by not reviewing any data and just asking how you can help them in their current role, you aren't limiting it to performance, you are asking a broader question that may reveal some interesting ways you as a leader can help support their development in their current role."

"Erik, why do you keep saying 'in their current role'?"

Elyse could see the passion Erik had for training after asking her follow-up question. Erik's eyes got bigger and brighter, his smile widened, and his hand gestures increased as the conversation dove deeper into the topic.

"Let me ask you a question, do you think all your sales reps are happy being in their current role for the rest of their lives?"

Elyse chuckled "I hope not, it would be great to see them grow within Mech Corp."

"Exactly! That is where the second topic begins. After you discuss how you can assist them in their current role, ask them 'How can I assist you in preparing for any roles within Mech Corp?' This will get them thinking about their future within our company however beyond their current role."

"What if they haven't thought about other roles or are too new to know what roles are available? What then?"

"You always want to encourage growth and development, however set proper expectations. When someone joins a company, they need to focus on learning their role before thinking about jumping into new opportunities. Ensuring all staff see a path of development is critical, so reviewing the potential future roles provides something for them to work towards and helps you as their leader support their growth."

With delight Elyse was quick to speak up, "I get it, so I ask them how I can help them in their current role, then I transition to how I can help them with future roles. My role is to provide development for now and for the future."

"Now you see how a one-on-one can still be focused on your team member's performance, however focused on what they feel they need from you as their leader rather than numbers and rankings. Let them drive the meeting, you are just there to keep it on the track and learn how you can best service them."

"Wait, you said there was three topics, we only went over two."

"The last one may come as a surprise; you want to ask them 'How can I help you develop for roles outside of our organization'."

Elyse was taken aback by the guidance Erik provided on this final topic. Why would we ever want to suggest staff leave Mech Corp?

"Hold up, why would I ask that, I don't want to lose any staff."

"I hear you, no one wants to lose staff, especially talented staff, however if you don't try and take sincere interest in developing your staff, you will lose them all the same. Be honest with yourself, do you feel everyone on your team wants to stay with Mech Corp their entire career?"

After a minute thinking about each of her team members, Elyse responded. "No, I don't think they all plan on retiring with Mech Corp."

"You are right! In fact, Mech Corp may not be the best fit for some of your team members now. That is not to say the skill sets you focus on will not be helpful in both their current and future roles, however helping each of your team members develop to their success will lead to a more engaged and higher performing team. When they achieve their goals, reach what they feel is success, it is a great feeling. You will want to help more staff and they will be more focused in their current role knowing they have your support while working towards a long-term fit. Also, it is the right thing to do! It is a great feeling helping someone grow."

Elyse was so engaged in the discussion, she realized she hadn't taken any notes. "Erik, hold on a second, I need to write this down." Elyse pulled out her notebook and started jotting down the key points about culture.

While Elyse was catching up on her thoughts, Erik took the time to step in with some sage advice. "Elyse, the key to making this style of one-on-one successful is setting the tone, which happens in your first one-on-one. In that first session you need to set the table, let your team member know the format and the three questions you will review each time. Be sure they know that at their next one-on-one you would like them to prepare their thoughts so you can start helping them right away. Additionally, on that first meeting get to know them, ask them about their life goals and build upon that. This is their time, not yours, be there to listen, advise and support as much as you can. Once you have learned how you can aid in their development, set a commitment to assist them and follow through. Some of your staff may not know what they want to do, just support them while they take the time to find their path."

Elyse was frantically writing, filling the pages of her notebook with the newfound insights. As she finished, a thought came to mind that must be addressed.

"But Erik, I don't have any new hires right now, how do I start this approach with staff I have already worked with and done a few one-on-ones?"

"That's simple, you can go back and re-establish expectations with your current staff, let them know you did some training of your own and would like to adjust your approach. I bet many of them would be happy to know you are investing in yourself."

Elyse smiled and the straightforward way she could implement this lesson.

"Oh my" Elyse exclaimed "Almost everyone is gone."

As they looked around the dining room, they realized dinner had ended with a few stragglers involved in conversations.

"Erik, I am going to call it a night, thank you for all your advice and guidance. I really appreciate you taking the time with me!"

"You are welcome, Elyse. Do me a favor, when you get back to your office, after you have tried this approach with a few of your staff's one-on-ones, call or email me so we can calibrate. I want to know how they are going so I can follow up with you and provide more guidance. One-on-ones are just part of the equation for developing your staff, once you master this we will move on to another lesson. I know you will do great!"

"I sure will. Thank you again Erik, have a great evening!"

As Elyse walked back to her room, she thought about how wonderful her first day was and all the lessons she had learned. She was grateful for the time Lisa and Erik spent with her and was optimistic that over the next three days she would be able to discover more on her journey to become a member of The Club.

Chapter 5: Knowledge

Elyse woke up on the second day with optimism and excitement. She had learned so much from two great leaders on the first day, the possibility to continue the learning today set the tone for her morning.

After getting ready for the day, she excitedly walked down to the daily continental breakfast, grabbed some fruit and a bagel with cream cheese and looked around the room to find a seat. Unlike the prior day, there weren't many people to start a discussion with as many of the Mech Corp leaders were not eating breakfast. Elyse found a corner seat and ate her breakfast alone and reviewed her notes from the prior day.

Once she had finished breakfast, Elyse reviewed the events of the day on the agenda which consisted of two options for each attendee at any time. Looking over the schedule she noticed there was a session in an hour that the top sales team leader, Steven Kingham, would be leading a session on product knowledge.

Thinking back to the opening night festivities and looking at her notes from that night, Steven mentioned knowledge as his key attribute to success. 'Maybe what he meant was product knowledge' Elyse thought to herself as she registered for the session and mapped out her day. Elyse knew the session he was hosting would be important in her journey.

An hour later Elyse was first in line to find a seat for Steven's session. As she entered the room, she noticed a stage set up with a single chair and a microphone. There didn't appear to be a screen or a whiteboard, she did not see any audio video staff to assist, just a simple set up. Elyse's interest was piqued as the topic of product knowledge seemed to be a complex one where she felt visuals would be helpful. After a few minutes passed for folks to find their seats, the spotlight turned on from stage left Steven walked out and sat down ready to start the session.

"Welcome all, I am so glad you are here to share this time and learn about my take on product knowledge. My name is Steven Kingham, I have been with Mech Corp for the past ten years, my first three years as a sales agent and the last seven as a sales manager with the Chicago branch. Before we get started, I want to share a brief fact about my career at Mech Corp that may provide some context to why this topic is a key factor in my team and my personal success."

"When I was a sales agent, I was not the best sales agent... in fact for the first two years I never consistently hit the goals of my role. You may be wondering, 'Steven if you weren't hitting your goals, how did you get to stay on staff for so long?

Steven paused while the audience gave a chuckle. Elyse was nodding her head up and down trying to understand how any sales manager would keep someone on their team who wasn't meeting goals consistently for that long.

"My manager cared about my success, and he worked with me every day to help me improve. Being so involved with my success, as he was with all the team members, he understood it took time to learn a role completely and was not interested in taking short cuts. I put in the effort, he observed that effort and stuck with me. During the time while I was learning the working towards my future potential, the one topic we constantly reviewed was product knowledge, and I was good at catching on to his methods."

"Another question that I often get is, how is it your team has been the top selling team the past five years? My response is always to have a focus on product knowledge. That product knowledge will drive quality conversations with each of your customers."

Elyse did not understand the path Steven was going down. Mech Corp prides itself on providing excellent new hire training to the sales agents and has a robust knowledge base where all products and specifications are outlined in detail. In addition to the detail of the products, the application of the products in the field along with relevant news articles were in place to aid the sales teams in their knowledge. In fact, Mech Corp had a few staff members at corporate who were responsible for updating the knowledge base, making it a key focal point for all sales agents and managers.

"I can see many of you are confused from my focus on product knowledge since we all know Mech Cor provides solid training and many tools for us to understand our product catalog. Even the setup of this room may cause concern knowing there are not visuals for us to reference."

"You see, the topic of our session today is 'Product Knowledge' not our products, rather a focus on our customers potential customers products. That is what I will be discussing with you all today."

The crowd became more silent as the realization hit that this session would be focused on an opportunity they had not realized.

"I want to make this session interactive, so I will be asking questions for you to consider for your branch. Many of the customers we have at the local level are unique to your area, so we will share some principles for applying the knowledge later in the session. Let's start with a moment of reflection, picture your largest customer in terms of revenue, what are their top three products or services?"

Elyse closed her eyes and thought about Jennings Electrical, the largest client within her team. She knew many of the components sold to Jennings were typically sold to hospitals and universities, however she was unsure about their most successful product or service. They had been customers for the past eight years and she inherited them when she was hired as a sales agent and once promoted the account was transferred to a sales agent on her staff. How could this be? How could she have overlooked something so obvious?

After a minute or two of silence, Steven looked up from his chair and asked a deafening question. "Who wants to share their best customer's bestselling product or service with the group?"

The crowd was silent, there were no volunteers. Everyone was looking at each other with the realization they were lacking the basic knowledge of their customers, the customers that they service every day, the customers that drive the growth of Mech Corp.

Steven chuckled and spoke up to calm the anxiety of the crowd. "It's ok to not know right now, show of hands how many of you will seek out this information and more about your customers when we leave this off-site?"

Every hand in the room went up, some even whistled or spoke up saying 'I will' and 'First thing when I get back to the office.' As the tenseness left the crowd as everyone needed this lesson, Steven continued.

"That is great! We have a great training program for our agents, and we mention knowing your customer, putting it into practice is different than speaking to the need. Now before we move on, I challenge you to each review this same question with your team members and work with them closely, so you and they all know the products that are successful for our customers. Next question, if you know what makes your customers successful, how can you apply that knowledge to help your sales team?"

Another pause in the presentation and another moment of thought. Elyse felt she knew the answer and raised her hand as if back in high school.

With a grin Steven pointed to Elyse and said, "Elyse from our Pittsburgh office, what are your thoughts?"

Elyse was stunned, how did Steven know who she was? They had not spoken before and there were over a hundred sales managers across Mech Corp. She stood up and in the strongest voice she could muster provided her thoughts to the crowd.

"I think if we know what makes our customers successful, we will be able to identify products that we have which can help them be more successful. A higher quality component to extend the life of their products or a part that meets specifications which costs less for services they provide."

"Both great suggestions Elyse, thank you! What else?" Steven asked the crowd.

Elyse sat down, her heart was racing, and she was too caught up to be aware of the next person's suggestions. She smiled with excitement knowing she contributed well to the conversation. Taking out her notebook, Elyse wrote down the few suggestions she provided. For a good portion of the session, Steven went around the room, calling on sales managers by name, listening to their specific suggestions and adding context when applicable. Elyse scribbled frantically until Steven moved the session along.

"All great suggestions team! In general, the more you know about your customers the more you can help align what we offer to assist them and if the situation arises where we can't be the company to help them, be honest and a good partner. Build the relationship with your customers and take a genuine interest in their business, keep them updated with the progress of our business, new products and check in without a fixed agenda."

Elyse was writing all of Steven's suggestions into her notebook as quickly as possible, trying not to miss any detail.

She looked up and the hour-long session had flown by with so many practical applications of this general principle.

"Product knowledge, regardless of it being our customers or our own internal products, is just one aspect of the general topic of knowledge that I spoke to briefly during our first night together. As leaders you must be curious about everything related to your team, your industry, and your success. The search for knowledge should drive you to new heights every day, and applying that knowledge is just as important as seeking it out. I want to thank you all for your time today and I hope you enjoy the rest of the off-site."

Steven was a performer; he knew how to leave his audience wanting more. As he closed his session the crowd stood up with great applause. Steven smiled and waved while walking off stage. Elyse was overjoyed to have chosen to sit in on this session, but a part of her felt there was something missing. She decided to stick around after the crowd left and approach Steven to see if she could get some more advice on the topic.

As Elyse walked up to the stage and peered around the corner, Steven was sitting down sipping water and resting from his enlightening session. She could see the passion Steven shared about this topic and decided to strike up a conversation.

"Hi Steven, thank you for an amazing lesson!"

"You are welcome, Elyse, I hope it helps you with your team and your branch."

Elyse smiled "I am sure it will, however I feel like there is something I can't put my finger on. How did you know so many of the leaders' names, including mine?"

Steven had a grin that showed he knew that what he demonstrated was impressive. "I used to be terrible at remembering names, so I have made it a point to focus on remembering the names of my peers. Prior to the session I looked at who registered for this session, and I went into the company resources to try and place faces to the names. If you are putting in the time to gain knowledge from me, I should put the time to address you by name."

"What if the crowd was twice the size, how would you remember all those names?" Elyse asked puzzled.

"I do my best, if you noticed I didn't know everyone's name and only used names when I was certain. I did not have a lot of time to learn them, but those who I was able to connect with on a name basis it created an impression, wouldn't you say?"

"I would say so!" Elyse responded with agreement. "Is that one of the ways you seek out knowledge?"

"I am a curious person; I like to learn, and I like to make people feel included. When I speak about seeking knowledge, it is all around us in so many ways. You can apply the principle to most any situation, in any industry. When selling any product or service, you must know about your customers and their needs. You must know your product or service and if there isn't a mutually beneficial fit then you will not build a lasting relationship. By putting in the time to know your customers, you can help them problem solve and find solutions to improve their business. Sometimes those solutions may not be with what you are selling, however that partnership will blossom, and remarkable things will bloom."

"Are you saying its ok to help our customers be successful even if we don't get the sale?"

"In short, yes. We need to do genuine good! Focus on doing the right thing and good things will happen. This isn't about your customers only, this is also about your staff, your family, your friends... anyone who you care about. Be curious and supportive, understand their situation and help wherever and whenever you are able."

Elyse stared at Steven for a moment while the advice settled in. After a moment of reflection, Elyse followed up with a comment about her feelings.

"I thought there was something I was missing from the session; I think what you just said fills that gap. I need to be knowledgeable about all things, sincerely curious and help even if there isn't anything in it for me. Does that sound right?"

"I couldn't have summarized it better myself" Steven said with a look of a proud parent of a student who just learned a valuable lesson. "If you understand how improving your understanding of the situation will help you grow while helping others achieve, it is a win-win!"

This advice was very refreshing, and Elyse was elated to have attended this session. "Thank you, Steven, for all your time, I deeply appreciate the advice. Out of curiosity, what session are you attending next?"

Steven chuckled "Well Elyse, I am attending the session on Customer Service. What are you registered for today?

"I haven't registered for the next one yet, I wanted to see how this one went first. I will consider that session, thank you for the great advice!"

"You are welcome, please continue to seek out knowledge, you will uncover many more lessons along the way. I am here if you ever want to talk shop."

As they parted ways, Elyse reflected on the morning events, she was well on her way to connecting with all the members of The Club. Before leaving the room, she jotted down the main points discussed with Steven in her notebook with a feeling of accomplishment.

Chapter 6: An Unlikely Ally

After jotting down her lessons from the first session of the day, Elyse looked at the remaining agenda for day two to determine her next session. Elyse noticed there was a session titled "Getting the Most Out of Every Day" and was being hosted by Monica Tan, one of The Club in a few hours.

Elyse thought about the topic Monica highlighted on that first evening, work ethic, she felt the session had to be connected and decided she would attend. With the a few hours to spare, Elyse decided to grab some lunch at the resort's café. As she walked in, she bumped into Jimmy from her home branch.

"Hi Jimmy" Elyse shouted with excitement!

"Afternoon Elyse" replied Jimmy. "You heading to lunch too?"

"You know it, want to join me?"

"That sounds great" Jimmy replied.

They sat down at a table together towards the rear of the room, both hungry, they perused the menu and exchanged small talk until the waiter addressed them. Jimmy was excited they had had a Cuban sandwich on the menu and ordered it quickly, Elyse decided to order a Grilled Chicken and Bacon sandwich. After ordering Elyse wanted to check in and see how Jimmy was feeling about the off-site.

"How is the off-site going for you Jimmy?"

Jimmy rolled his eyes and let out a long sigh before responding. "You know, it is what I expected. Everyone in leadership is trying to get the rest of us to buy into the vision. Same as always."

There was a long pause as Elyse needed time to process Jimmy's statement. This was her first off-site, and she was learning so much, soaking in each lesson like a sponge and grateful Mech Corp was hosting this event for their sales leaders to grow.

"What do you mean Jimmy?" Elyse asked with a curious tone.

Jimmy smiled "Don't mind me Elyse, I am sure there is a lot of positives for someone like you at events like this."

This statement was concerning Elyse, how did Jimmy think they were different? Immediately Elyse knew she had to keep asking questions to discover what led Jimmy to feel this way.

"Someone like me?"

"Yeah, you are new to leadership, I have been in this role for five years. After doing the same thing over and over for five years with the same lack luster results, never being a top performer is frustrating and these sessions just become noise. If I had the opportunity to turn back time things may be different, however now I attend the off-site as a requirement not as a choice."

Elyse was stunned. Jimmy had given up on the possibility of being great at his role. She thought if he accepted a role in leadership, he had to have wanted to lead a team and be thriving at some point, what could have happened to cause him to feel this way?

"What happened to make you feel this way?"

Jimmy smiled for a moment as Elyse could see he was recalling memories over the past five years. After a brief silence Jimmy shared his experience with Elyse.

"Back then we were a smaller branch, Susan was the only manager until I was promoted, and the team was split in two. That off-site when I was a manager was hosted in Baltimore, so we decided to make it a road trip. It was about a four-hour drive give or take a stop or two. When I jumped in the car, I was excited to learn and grow, heck I thought I could make it to 'The Club' the following year. On the drive, Susan filled me in on how the off sites of the past were, how it was a bunch of propaganda to highlight those who lucked their way into 'The Club' or were 'favorites' of the higher ups and to just enjoy the time away from work. From that point on I had dark lenses on, and each speech, each team building, and each session was nothing more than rhetoric."

At that moment Elyse could see Jimmy was reflecting on his past as he never had before. There was a small light in his eye that had been dimmed for years and that faint glow needed to be fanned into a fire. Elyse knew exactly what to do.

"I am so sorry to hear you feel that way Jimmy. You know this is my first off-site, I want to be part of 'The Club' next year. I have learned a lot these past few days and hope to keep learning and using those lessons to help my team improve.

Even if I do not make it next year, what I have discovered will help my team members. I will not give up. You should not give up on yourself."

Jimmy looked up with a smile, realizing that the greenest manager at their Pittsburgh branch just brough a glimmer of hope to his future. "You really believe that don't you?"

"Absolutely!" Elyse exclaimed with enthusiasm. "While it may look like rhetoric and propaganda to others, I see a lot of lessons all around us… and the lesson you just taught me was to always form my own opinion. I received similar feedback when I asked about what to expect at this off-site to what you described, but I did not let that cloud my judgement. I went into it with open eyes, and I am glad I did. You should see what I have already learned, and we still have two days left!"

Elyse opened her notebook in the direction of Jimmy so he could see the high-level takeaways from the past two days.

"Jimmy, if you have a desire and the will then there is always time to make a change in yourself and to help make a positive change in others. Don't give up on yourself."

Jimmy looked at Elyse and spoke in a quiet humble tone; "You are right Elyse. Thank you for helping me see some light again."

With a large smile Elyse nodded her head slightly to acknowledge Jimmy's thanks.

"I have an idea, I am heading to Monica's session soon, why don't you join me? We can sit together and listen to what she has to say. She accomplished what you set out to do before the road trip and what I hope to accomplish next year."

"Oh yeah, what is that?"

"She has only been a manager for one year and made 'The Club', if anyone has some insight into what it takes, I bet she does."

Jimmy chuckled, "That sounds like a great idea, happy to join you. Let's get there first to get good seats."

With that, they finished their lunch and were on their way.

Chapter 7: Work Ethic

Elyse and Jimmy were among the first sales leaders at the session. They found seats in the center of the front row, as this session was in a smaller room than some of the other sessions. Elyse thought since Monica was new there may not be as many managers attending her session.

Soon others started to fill the room and before long the room was filled, by the time the session started it was standing room only. In all there were about forty managers in a room that appeared to only seat twenty-five.

Just then Monica stepped out on stage, only her and a microphone. Monica appeared to be a lifelong professional, dressed in a nice business suit with a presence that commanded the attention of the room. Everyone went silent in anticipation of her opening statement.

"Hi everyone!" Monica stated in a Boston accent with enthusiasm. "It looks like we ran out of room for everyone to fit. I have an idea! There are some chairs up here on the side of the stage, why don't those without chairs come up here and get one, and those of you who have a chair let's make room, so everyone is comfortable?"

Without any questions or hesitation, everyone in the back of the room walked to the front and got a chair and everyone in the audience moved their row up a little so another row could be made in the back. Elyse watched this in awe, how could this room full of different people come together so quickly? What was it about Monica's presence that demanded such quick devotion?

Monica smiled while everyone made the adjustments, then she spoke, "Nice work everyone, let's give ourselves a round of applause."

Again, like clockwork, everyone started to clap and smile. Jimmy looked at Elyse with wonder as to how the group got together so quickly.

"I am so happy to see so many wonderful leaders at this session. I must admit I was a bit worried no one would show up. My name is Monica Tan, I am a Boston native, and I started with Mech Corp as a sales manager last year. I am having so much fun working for an amazing company and with a wonderful team. Speaking of team, show of hands how many of you feel your team drives your success?"

Monica paused for a moment as most of the hands in the room were raised.

Elyse looked at Jimmy who had his hand raised and she raised her hand, without her team she would not be able to accomplish anything. Then Elyse looked around the room and all the sales managers had their hands up.

With a large grin, Monica addressed the crowd again, "Thank you... if you can hand down" as she motioned for the crowd to reset for another question. "Now, how many of you feel you are the drivers of your team's success?"

This time when Elyse scanned the room there were few hands in the air. She thought about the question for a moment then raised her hand with enthusiasm.

"Well now" Monica exclaimed as she starred directly at Elyse sitting front and center in the audience. "Your hand went up twice, stand up, tell us your name, which branch you are from and why you had your hand raised both times?"

Being a sales manager, Elyse was not shy, however standing up in front of the group to answer Monica's question triggered a lump in her throat. Elyse stood up, turned around and mustered up her clearest loud voice to ensure everyone could hear.

"My name is Elyse; I am a sales manager from the Pittsburgh branch. I raised my hand for the first question because without my team being successful then I would not be successful. It took me a moment to raise my hand on the second question because I wondered how I impact them, then I realized what I do helps them be successful too."

Elyse sat down. Jimmy patted her on the arm to show a job well done. Elyse was now laser focused on Monica and eager to hear what was next.

With a charming smile, Monica addressed Elyse directly. "Thank you, often we as leaders question the impact we have on our staff. Our purpose as leaders is to ensure we are empowering our teams to get the most out of each day. With that in mind, the focal point of our discussion today is work ethic. Can anyone tell me what work ethic is?"

Every hand in the room went up, Elyse had rarely seen an audience so willing to participate. It was amazing to see so many of her peers share the eagerness to learn. Monica pointed to a sales manager towards the back.

"How about you there in the nice brown suit jacket. Tell us your name, what branch you are from and what you believe work ethic to be?"

A tall man with blond hair and a golden tan stood up to address the crowd. "My name is Chase; I am from the San Jose branch and happy to be here with all of you. Work ethic is being able to focus on the work that needs to be done until it is complete, pushing yourself to ensure it gets done. Sometimes it has to do with working hard long hours and other times it may be working smart, just keep at it until the job is done."

"Thank you, Chase. That is a detailed definition. Let's get a few more descriptions of work ethic. Hi there, tell us your name, branch and how would you describe work ethic?" Monica repeated as she pointed to a woman sitting on the left end of the first row.

"Hi everyone, my name is Missy. I am from the Santa Fe branch. Work ethic has to do with being accountable for your job duties and for helping others. Work ethic involves doing the right things and setting an example for others."

"Thank you, Missy, again a thorough explanation of work ethic. Let's get one more opinion. How about you there, in the middle row with the red dress on? Can you tell us your name, branch and what you feel work ethic is all about?"

"Hello all, my name is Kelsey, I am from the Atlanta branch. Work ethic comes down to being honest and doing what you are doing what you are supposed to be doing while you are supposed to be doing it."

"Wow that is a mouthful, thank you Kelsey for another solid description of work ethic. Nice work everyone! You are all correct, there are so many ways we can interpret work ethic from focusing on work duties while at work, working harder and smarter, being accountable and responsible are just a few descriptors. Let's answer another question, show of hands, how many of you would like to improve your personal work ethic?"

The crowd was bought into whatever Monica was selling, every hand in the room went up without question. Even Jimmy was on the edge of his seat eager to learn more.

"That is great, one more question, how many of you would like to improve your team's overall work ethic?"

Again, every hand went back up in a furry. Elyse thought to herself who wouldn't want a team who works harder and smarter with accountability for results.

"Great, then you will want to learn this simple lesson."

Standing on stage with only a microphone and her huge personality, Monica held up a small circular shaped object. It would have been difficult to see from the back of the room, however Elyse had a front row seat, turned to Jimmy with confusion, and said, "Jimmy is that a gum band?"

Jimmy nodded and smiled while shrugging his shoulders to show his confusion.

"You all know what this is, it is a rubber band!"

The crowd, which was eager and enthusiastic hushed to show their anticipation for an explanation.

Monica stood on the stage with a large grin, knowing she owed more details to the audience. "You see this rubber band represents the inherent work ethic in all of us. We learn this work ethic from our family, from our upbringing and from our experiences. Now you may not realize this, but rubber bands are stretchy."

A small chuckle echoed in the room as Monica paused for effect. "You see you can stretch the rubber band a little, and it goes right back to being the same size." Monica was now pacing the stage slightly stretching the rubber band. "If you keep stretching it, little by little each day, eventually it will be a bit larger when it is not being stretched. As you continue to stretch it, the rubber band will get slightly more pliable and will still retain its shape and retain its ability to function."

"Now what happens if I stretch this thing this far?" Just then Monica began stretching the rubber band well beyond its limits. While doing so you heard some folks in the audience yell 'It will break' and just like that the rubber band broke in Monica's hands.

"You got it, it breaks. This is a visual representation of how you need to treat yourself and your teams when you are seeking to improve work ethic, which will lead to getting more out of each day. Focus on incremental improvements that will make a long-lasting difference rather than trying to stretch yourself and your team so far that you cannot manage the work. If you focus on those steps to improvement, it will take time however the results will be long lasting."

Elyse pulled out her notebook, she was so caught up in the engagement of the presentation she had almost forgotten to add to her previous lessons.

"Let me give you a real-life work example. We all want our newly hired sales agents to hit the ground running. Your newest team member just graduated training and shadowed your top sales agent for the past two weeks. It is time for them to be on their own. You set a goal for them to find and reach out to twenty prospects, conduct four sales visits and close one sale in their first week. How many of you have set similar first week goals?"

Elyse looked at Jimmy who had raised his hand in response to the question. As she looked around the room most of the hands were raised, affirming Monica's week one goals.

"We set these three goals, the new sales agent is working as hard as they can however are unable to set up the four visits, they have found fifteen prospects and are focused on finding the other five, where the actual goal of closing one sale this week has slipped their mind. We have focused them on the actions of the process more so than the outcome. Did we set this person up for success? No... we set them up for discouragement and failure."

Elyse, being a new manager, understood both sides of this example. When she was a new hire, she had a similar week one expectation and she failed miserably for many weeks, eventually she got her first sale and started to work smarter. She also thought of her most recent new hire and how she had pushed him to do the same, focus on outreach, and like her he had failed. She turned her attention back to Monica.

"We have all either been there and that is ok. We all know the sales funnel and should work with our staff on improving skills to make the funnel from outreach to sale shorter. We want them to follow the process in a compliant way. We owe it to our staff to coach and develop them and help them focus on the right outcome, after all learning is part of the journey."

Monica continued, "You know, sometimes it works out and the agent meets the outreach and sales goal, so we immediately ask for more, now one hundred and fifty prospects, eight sales pitches and two sales. This turns into more because we are playing catch up for others' missed goals with staff who are meeting goals. This causes a gap; newer staff may become unhappy in their role because they are being pushed too hard too fast. Others become disengaged and start looking elsewhere for an environment that makes them feel supported and successful. Others keep trying and trying and trying and eventually burn out. As leaders we are responsible for stretching each staff member's skill sets responsibly, like the rubber band."

There was a pause around the room as every sales manager took inventory of these relevant examples while Monica walked from one side to side of the stage to the other.

"As a leader, it is important to know our actions have impacts on people, specifically their work ethic. Some of us have made the same mistake we just reviewed with our newly hired staff members. Now that we have recognized our mistake, what can we do to learn and grow?"

"Let us take that same situation and strip down the goal to simply making one sale. That is, it, get your first sale. Your new hire went through the training, shadowed your agents, you hired them for a reason, let them succeed. That is not to say you don't check in on the process and verify they are working hard towards that sale. Ask them open-ended questions about their progress, their sourcing and how you can help. Be supportive! When they schedule their first appointment go with them. If you are unable to ride along, send a seasoned agent to mentor them."

"Eventually, they will need to go at it alone, but make sure they start feeling supported, this will help build lasting results. Praise them for their incremental improvements and celebrate their wins."

Monica paused for a moment of reflection, while Elyse continued taking notes, hanging on every word.

"If we focus our efforts on the right outcomes and on improving our agent's skill set each day, we are building a work ethic within each of them that will be sustainable. If you stay true and focus on those little improvements the results will last. Thank you all for your time today!"

Monica paused to take a sip of water, parched from talking so much, then she bowed and walked off the stage. The crowd began to clap loudly in appreciation for the simple, yet impactful lesson.

Elyse finished writing and looked over at Jimmy who two days ago had felt negatively about this off-site and his prospects within his role. Jimmy was smiling and had a renewed look on his face.

"Well, what did you think?" Elyse asked Jimmy with a tone that echoed 'I told you so'.

"Thank you, Elyse. You helped me go into this session with open eyes and for the first time in a long time I feel engaged. I have a lot of self-reflection to do, I know I can make an impact. When we get back to home base could we work together to help both our teams?"

Elyse could see a sparkle in his eye and felt accomplished that she helped Jimmy find some light in what was a seemingly a tough situation. "Of course, Jimmy, we can work on this together!" she expressed with bright eyes and eagerness.

"I am heading to my room to rest up, thank you again Elyse, I will be sure to make the most of our remaining time here at the off-site. Catch up with you soon."

Elyse remained seated, reviewing her notes, and reflecting on the past few days. She had accomplished eighty percent of her objective. She had learned about culture, knowledge, development, and work ethic. Only one more topic remained on her list and only one more day.

Elyse felt an additional sense of success as she had positively impacted Jimmy. After a long day ed as she picked up her things and decided to spend the rest of the evening in her room relaxing.

Chapter 8: Motivation

Waking up on the final day of the off-site, Elyse felt excitement, urgency, and a sense of worry. This was her last day with all her peers, away from the day-to-day requirements of her role. The night before she was so exhausted, she did not have an opportunity to view the remaining agenda before falling asleep. In fact, thinking back, she doesn't remember much after eating a light dinner in her room. Before heading out for the day, Elyse reviewed her notes and made it a point to focus on the final topic, motivation, the only one she did not have the chance to explore. This was the topic Javier spoke of on the first night, she was curious to see if he would be hosting a session.

Elyse opened the agenda and immediately noticed a team building exercise this morning which at first glance looked like a trust fall, something she had always wanted to try. She looked at the other options in the morning and decided she would certainly go to the trust fall exercise. Reviewing the agenda after lunch there were a limited number of options; one session titled 'Building Standard Operating Procedures for Success' and another session titled 'Optimization and You' and a third option 'Staying Up to Date on Product Specs.' None of these looked to fill the void in her list.

Elyse decided she would have time during lunch to determine the rest of the day. The off-site concluded with a formal dinner at seven before flying back to Pittsburgh the next morning.

She wondered how to conclude her journey, she still had not discussed motivation with Javier. Elyse thought about scheduling a call with Javier when she returned. She started to worry about his busy schedule and the time she would need to implement the many lessons she had learned. Elyse shook away the feelings of worry and decided to focus on the immediate.

To prepare for the first session, Elyse readied herself with the required athletic shoes and casual clothes. As she walked to the first session, she took a moment to soak in the scenery for the first time while in San Diego. The smell of the ocean, which was only a few miles away, and the warm bright sun, something she did not see frequently enough at home. This moment of simplicity provided her with a sense of confidence. She had accomplished so much these past few days, however the sense of not completing her journey weighed heavy in her mind.

The first session was exactly as she had imagined, there was a large turnout of sales managers who were engaging in a very safe yet aptly named "trust fall" exercise. While this was exciting, fun, and lasted most of the morning, all Elyse could think about was seeking out the knowledge she was lacking to complete her list. This list was a road map to being part of 'The Club' next year!

At lunch, Elyse found herself sitting alone, not by design rather as a symptom of her singular focus. Her typical outgoing self was more reserved as the internal pressure to complete her lessons was mounting. 'How could I have come this far' she thought 'There has to be a way.' A moment later her thought process changed; 'You have learned so much, you shouldn't be this hard on yourself, there are a lot of valuable lessons to take away.'

As the lunch break continued, her thoughts teetered back and forth between gratitude for the lessons learned and a longing for that final topic. Elyse was getting up to leave when she noticed Javier gesturing salutations to the table he had just left. Without a plan, thought or reservation, Elyse sprang up and started to follow Javier out of the café.

Javier, a tall thin man with a long stride, was getting away from Elyse as he walked down a scenic garden path. Elyse increased her speed to a fast walk, wondering if what she was doing was borderline creepy. After a minute she got close enough to speak up without yelling. "Javier" she said slightly out of breath.

At that moment Javier stopped and turned around with a look of confusion and noticed a smiling woman fast walking towards him. "Hi, how can I help you?" Javier said, confused as to who was following him and why.

Elyse stopped as she approached Javier, put her hands on her hips and took a deep breath before speaking.

"Hi Javier, my name is Elyse, a sales manager at the Pittsburgh branch. I really appreciated your topic of motivation, and I was hoping you had a few minutes to talk."

Without hesitation Javier replied, "Hi Elyse from the Pittsburgh branch. I have a few minutes to talk about motivation."

Elyse quickly started to explain herself. "You see, I am new to management, and I want to be part of 'The Club' next year. I have met with all the other members of this year's 'Club' these past few days, and you are the only one I have not had a chance to learn from. On our first night when you were up on stage, you mentioned motivation as a key reason for your success, I was hoping you could provide some details and tips on how I can motivate others."

Javier looked at Elyse and a smile came over him, overjoyed to have someone interested in a topic so important, "May I ask, what motivated you to want to be a member of The Club?"

Elyse froze, she did not expect any questions. "I think it would be great to be recognized for a job well done and seen by my peers as the best. It would mean that my team was successful and that I played a significant role in their success."

"How would that make you feel to know that you were seen as the best and that your team was successful?" Javier asked.

"I would feel accomplished to be held in high recognition by my peers and I would feel proud of my team."

Javier smiled and continued to ask questions. "Tell me Elyse, if you didn't make 'The Club', but your team was still successful, enjoying their job, working towards their future goals and career ambitions, would you still be proud of them?"

This was a deep question, but a simple one for Elyse. "Yes, I would still be proud of them. I see the arduous work they do day in and day out and I feel that now. I would totally be happy for them!"

"I see, so the true difference between being in 'The Club' and not being in 'The Club' is your own sense of accomplishment then, right?"

Elyse stopped for a second and thought about Javier's statement, after some thought spoke up. "I guess it would be my own personal accomplishment, is that wrong?"

"Not at all. It just means you have an internal drive to feel accomplished. You jogged down this path, following an unfamiliar peer into a garden just to ask him his thoughts on motivation. You clearly have the motivation you need to be successful!"

Elyse's eyes lit up and she realized what this brief interaction with Javier was, it was his way of showing Elyse how to understand her motivation. She had to know more.

"Wait, it isn't that simple, is it?"

"I wouldn't say it is simple, I would say if you were talking with someone who is motivated and knows what genuinely drives them, then it is not as difficult to help your staff embrace motivation. Some of your staff may not be self-aware of their motivations and others may not be willing to dive deep enough to understand. In your case, you were quick to get to the point of your motivation, the feeling of being in 'The Club', simply a sense of accomplishment."

"Wow" Elyse said with amazement. "How do you motivate others? I get understanding my motivation, how do I motivate others?"

"You must help each of your team members find their internal motivation. It is not about driving your team to motivation; sure, you can have pep rallies and gimmicks to try and motivate them in the short term. You can also use compensation, which may create an effect of them expecting compensation to work harder in the future. If you genuinely want lasting results, you need to help your staff find their motivation and you must know what motivates them."

Javier continued, "For example, have you ever asked a member of your team what motivates them?"

"Yes" Elyse responded as she could think of a few of these conversations with her staff.

"Great, did you ask them what that money does for them? What does that mean to them?"

"Sorry, I don't understand, money allows you to buy stuff and have a better lifestyle, provide for others, why would I ask them what money does for them?"

Javier had a look on his face that Elyse read as a teacher getting ready for an eye-opening lesson. "Those are all things you can do with money, yes, what does it do for that employee? For example, if someone says it allows me to have a better lifestyle, ask them to tell you about that lifestyle and what it means for them."

Javier continued, "They may say it allows them to travel, then you ask what they enjoy about traveling, you keep digging in until you get the feeling behind what the money does for them. Sometimes it will be a feeling of security, sometimes the feeling may be pride in their ability to provide for their family, others may be a sense of peace knowing they save money for their child's college fund. Find their internal motivation and then help them reach their goals."

Elyse stood there thinking deeply about her team, and how at this moment she realized she may not know them as well as she thought. One specific sales agent who works on Elyse's team came to mind.

"Javier, does everyone have internal motivation? There is a member of my team who does not talk much about his personal life, and I don't know if he is motivated, any thoughts on what I could do?"

"Sometimes people do not share their feelings right away. It could be you have not built enough trust with him, or he is just very private. One thing I wouldn't do is give up. If you sincerely want to help him, find his motivation, be genuine and sincere, he will eventually come around."

Elyse realized now, she was looking at motivation as a tool for her team to achieve, however a person's true motivation may not be the specific goals of their job. Elyse always felt her team knew she wanted them to be successful, had she not differentiated their specific success versus the team's goals?

"I need to write this down" Elyse said as she pulled out her notebook and started jotting down her revelations about motivation.

"Can I see what you have learned these last few days?" Javier said with interest.

"Sure!" Elyse exclaimed as she handed Javier her notes over the past few days.

"I am impressed, a lot of great nuggets of wisdom here. I must get to the next session; it was nice meeting you and thank you for the conversation. I hope to see you up on that stage next year."

With that Javier continued his walk. Elyse meandered over to a nearby bench to sit down and take it all in. She did it! She connected with each 'Club' member and had many lessons to implement with her team. After a few moments of reflection, she stood up and took in another big breath of the ocean air, looked up at the blue sky and started her way back to her room to prepare for the final event of the off-site, the formal dinner.

Chapter 9: The Formal Dinner

Elyse was in her room, getting ready for the formal dinner, she was not keen on having to formally dress, however her accomplishments of the past few days gave her more confidence.

As she was leaving her room, she bumped into her friend Lee Tate. Lee was part of the new hire class with Elyse in Pittsburgh as a sales agent, however transferred to the Philadelphia branch to be closer to her family a few months into the role. Both Elyse and Lee had worked hard and made it to the role of sales manager quickly within Mech Corp. Elyse was surprised they had not run into each other over the past few days.

"Hi Lee" beamed Elyse with outstretched arms!

Lee gave Elyse a big hug "Hi E, it has been great! How about for you?"

"Going great, learning a lot from the formal sessions and from networking with other branch leaders!"

"I know" replied Lee, "it seems like a new lesson around every corner, I can't wait to get back and put some of it to action."

"Agreed" Elyse exclaimed, "and who knows maybe we will both be part of 'The Club' next year!"

"Wouldn't that be something!" Lee responded with ambition in her eyes and a bright smile.

As they walked towards the formal hall, they heard soft jazz playing and as they entered immediately noticed the illuminated Mech Corp logo ice sculpture. The room was large and dimly lit with circular tables that seated eight. Unlike the kick-off Platinum Performer Presentation, the formal dinner had assigned seating with branches who were close together sitting together, a pleasant surprise for both Elyse and Lee.

After settling down at their table, the two looked around and noticed the men, most wearing business suits, vests, and fancy shoes. Women were dressed in different evening wear, some in suits, some in long flowing dresses and others in shimmery sweaters and slacks. They were the first at their table, however, were shortly joined by Susan and Jimmy from the Pittsburgh branch, Linda and Tim from the Philadelphia branch and Damon and Jacob from the Baltimore branch.

The sales leaders at Mech Corp continued to file in, finding their assigned table and gawking at the lavishness of the event. The servers were extremely attentive, bringing out water, taking drink orders and helping to seat all the guests. The walls had lighting accents of white, blue, and purple, the Mech Corp colors, providing a trendy ambiance. On stage a jazz band played at just the right volume. In the center of the stage was a draped screen with the Mech Corp logo displayed and a podium front and center.

Promptly at seven, Peter Lytle took the stage again. The room started to quiet down in anticipation of both his words of wisdom and the upcoming dinner.

"Good evening team!" Peter stated with a booming confident voice. "Thank you all for making this year's off-site a wild success." With that, he stepped away from the podium, walked around the stage and began clapping as everyone joined in, some whistling and voicing their excitement.

"He really knows how to get the crowd going huh?" Lee said to Elyse.

"Yeah, he really does, wonder if that is natural or comes with years of experience, maybe a little of both" Elyse replied as they returned their attention to the stage.

"Historically we have always kicked-off our annual off-site by celebrating the members of each year's 'Club'. The main reason we do this is to provide those of you who strive to be the best for our company, for yourselves and most importantly for your teams some additional focus from the jump."

"Our 'Club' members do not know they have won until they arrive at our off-site, however when they check in, they are notified, sworn to secrecy, and instructed to consider the one specific skill they felt helped them lead their team to success and achieve this impressive accomplishment. We do this so they are not caught off guard on stage and for so purposeful thought to be put into their choice. This then allows other to reflect on those skills as we progress through the off-site."

Elyse felt Peter was talking directly to her. Since that first night she was determined to learn as much about what the 'The Club' members had highlighted. She thought to herself that if this was the purpose of the ceremony on that first night, they nailed it!

"Over the years, sometimes the skills outlined fit nicely with the sessions we have planned and other times they do not, however that does not reduce their importance. We have seen trends over the years and this year was no exception. Without fail skills such as building culture, developing your employees, having solid work ethics, enhancing your team's knowledge, and building culture have echoed over and over."

"I know that each of you have taken away many lessons from our limited time together, I ask that you take one more. Do not let perfection stop you from your own personal growth, focus on incremental improvement over delayed perfection and you will go far. Start now as there is no time like the present and reach as far as you want to go!"

The crowd erupted in applause for these final words of wisdom. Peter was on stage clapping and smiling with pride. Elyse could see the joy in his eyes as he surveyed the room, knowing the effort put into this event was impactful to many.

"While we enjoy each other's company and partake in this delicious meal, let's reflect on some memories of this event. Play the slide show!" With that, Peter stepped down from the stage, the lights dimmed around the stage and the screen lit up as the Jazz Band continued to play. A slide show of pictures from the off-site flashed on the screen.

The servers began to bring out the meals while sales leaders reacted to some pictures captured of the memories of the off-site. Peter walked around spending a few minutes at each table. When he arrived at Elyse's table, everyone stopped eating and gazed up with appreciation.

"How is everyone's night going" he said with his usual charm.

"Everything is great" Elyse stated, taking charge, and speaking on behalf of the table.

"Elyse, right?"

"Yeah" Elyse replied astonished that Peter remembered her name from his Pittsburgh visit.

"I heard you have been tracking down members of 'The Club' to learn from them, even going as far as following them down garden paths? Should I be worried?" Peter said with a grin.

Slightly embarrassed, Elyse responded with an affirmative nod. "No need to worry, I was trying to learn as much as possible from the members of 'The Club'. After lunch I observed Javier walking away, he was the last one I needed to connect with, so I flagged him down."

"Well, that is some true ambition. I hope you found what you were looking for!"

"I did, I learned a lot this week, thank you for hosting this, I can't wait for next year!"

Peter smiled "Me too Elyse, me too. Enjoy your evening all, I will be back around soon."

"Who did you stalk through a garden?" Lee asked with a puzzled look.

"Javier Santos" Elyse said with a chuckle. "He was the last 'Club' member I needed to speak with. You see, on that first night I jotted down the five traits they shared and made it a point to learn about those five points from the five 'Club' members. It was a challenge, but I did it!"

Just then Elyse pulled out her notebook and showed it to Lee. Once Lee finished reviewing it, she handed it to Jimmy who continued to pass it around the table for everyone to see.

"That is so you, striving to be the best, just like our time in training" Lee added.

"What can I say, I want my team to succeed so I can join 'The Club' next year." Elyse said beaming with pride.

Elyse put her notebook back in her purse and felt at peace, she had accomplished the task, met many new people, reconnected with some old friends, and had a list of solid actions to aid in her team development. As the night continued her feelings of success grew stronger with a desire to get back to her branch, back to her team to start making an impact!

Chapter 10: One Year Later

"Welcome all! Today we reflect on our accomplishments, how we have achieved them and met our goals this past year." Peter Lytle was back on stage welcoming the sales leaders to the event, this year in Dallas.

Elyse was sitting with her fellow Pittsburgh branch sales manager Jimmy, both were clapping and engaged, getting ready for yet another productive off-site. Both had worked hard this past year, improving the Pittsburgh branch to being in the top ten across the organization.

"This has to be your year" Jimmy exclaimed to Elyse, who began to blush. "Have they pulled you aside, do you know something?"

Elyse smiled, "Oh Jimmy, we shall see!" turning back to focus on Peter and his opening address. Elyse and Jimmy had a much closer connection since the last off-site. Jimmy had been more positive, and it has paid off. The past year was Jimmy's most successful since becoming a sales manager. His team was more engaged, his attitude towards the role had drastically improved, and he and Elyse were working together more closely.

"This past year has been some ride, if not this year next year; for both of us!" Jimmy replied with confidence in his voice and a suspicious look. "It is a shame Susan isn't here with us" he stated with slight sarcasm.

The prior month Susan had decided sales leadership at Mech Corp was not the right fit for her and decided to make a career change to retail sales. Elyse was happy Susan was moving into a career she felt was more of a fit. She thought about a year ago when she heard Susan's opinion of toff-site. She was glad that conversation did not negatively influence her.

"Tonight, I want you all to reflect on how your role as a leader has an impact on the success of your team. Think about that impact on meeting organizational goals and the relationships you share with our business partners and customers. I hope you each take the chance at our off-site to build upon your skill sets and are ready to learn new lessons. With that, thank you for being here as a leadership family."

Just like last year, Peter was on theme, ensuring his message was consistent.

"Last year was a momentous year at Mech Corp. Our revenue exceeded fifty million, another profitable year! We had an explosive sales year, bringing on over one thousand new customers across all our locations. Customer Retention was again up year over year, a testimonial to the hard work and dedication of you and your teams."

The room filled with cheers and applause; Elyse was energized by the positivity. Like prior years, the sales leadership team had exceeded expectations, certainly a reason to celebrate.

"While our sales teams met or outperformed, we take this opportunity to recognize the top five sales teams from the past year. Without further delay, it is my pleasure to announce this year's Platinum Performer Club Members!"

"Our first member of this year's Platinum Club is also our top sales team leader each of the last six years! This past year he again broke previous sales record and set another new ceiling for Mech Corp, from our Chicago branch; Steven Kingham!"

Elyse was so happy to see Steven back up on stage. Elyse began meeting with Steven monthly after the last off-site. At first it was a continuation of the lesson on product knowledge, however they morphed into leadership think tanks, helping one another talk through ways to improve their impact on their teams.

"Our next member is also no stranger to this stage, in her second year with Mech Corp she has yet again made it to The Club, leading our company in customer satisfaction scores for two years in a row, please celebrate from our Boston branch Monica Tan!"

The crowd roared as Elyse reflected on the last off-site and the way Monica owned the room during her presentation. While they had not connected much in the past year, that one session had left an impression.

"The third member of our club this year has been with Mech Corp for eleven years now and is a repeat winner, three times in the last six years and two years in a row. Hailing from our Nashville branch, Lisa Townsley!"

Lisa and Elyse had remained in contact after the last off-site, thinking back it was her initial conversation with Lisa that provided the extra spark she needed to follow through.

"Being a newcomer to this club is no small feat, this year we have two new members. Both started their Mech Corp careers as a sales agent and worked their way up into leadership and both reside in the Keystone State, please give it up for Lee Tate from our Philadelphia branch and Elyse Jones from our Pittsburgh branch!"

Jimmy looked over at Elyse as she stood up and gave him a wink, radiant with excitement. Elyse looked around and found Lee who was walking towards the stage. They both found out when they arrived, as Peter had outlined the last year, to give them time to think about the specific skill that helped them the last year. As she glided to the stage, the overwhelming feeling of accomplishment came over her again, this time with more vigor than her earlier notification of winning. Her peers cheering her on, the atmosphere of the event and seeing Peter welcoming her with open arms on stage as a member of 'The Club'.